TO

FROM

DATE

ONE SOLITARY LIFE

Based on the noted passage by

James Allan Francis

With commentary by

Ken Blanchard

In partnership with

Mac Anderson

COUNTRYMAN

Nashville, Tennessee

ONE SOLITARY LIFE

Design: Koechel Peterson & Associates, Inc. | Minneapolis, Minnesota

ISBN 1 4041 0172 1 | Printed and bound in the United States of America

www.thomasnelson.com | www.jcountryman.com

"You are great, O Lord GOD.

For there is none like You,

nor is there any God besides You."

2 SAMUEL 7:22 NKJV

One Solitary Life is one of the most inspiring stories I know. I'll never forget the first time I heard it read. It was at the end of the Christmas pageant at the Crystal Cathedral in Orange, California, at a time when my faith was reawakening after a long slumber.

My mom and dad had been great fans of Robert Schuller and his "Hour of Power." From the moment they tuned into his very first televised Sunday service several decades ago, my parents were hooked on the positive philosophy and faith that Robert Schuller espoused. In fact, if you made a sound during Sunday's "Hour of Power" you were in trouble, because that was a very special time of the week for them.

In 1978 my dad was suffering from cancer. I brought him and my mom out to California for Christmas. It was a wonderful time to be with him, with family gathered around. Dad made it through the holidays but died early in February. That March my mom was still with us. One Sunday I said to her, "You've never seen Reverend Schuller live, have you?" And she said, "No, Dad and I always watched him on TV." I said, "Let's go up today." So we drove up to Orange County for the "Hour of Power." That day was the last service in the old chapel.

Halfway through the service the whole congregation got up and marched into the new Crystal Cathedral. It was extraordinary to be there for this grand opening. Reverend Schuller's sermon that day was entitled "Every Ending Is a New Beginning." My mom said to me, "Can you imagine Reverend Schuller designing a sermon just for me? There are no accidents in life."

During that service I turned to my mom and said, "Someday, Mom, I'm going to be up there with Reverend Schuller." She said, "Really?" I said, "Yes, I don't know how, but I just get a feeling that I'll be there." It was four years later—after *The One Minute Manager*® came out—that I stood with Reverend Schuller in the Crystal Cathedral, with my mom in the congregation. That was when I began to look closely at my faith. I had turned my back on the Lord for over fifteen years, but the success of *The One Minute Manager* was so absurd that even I had trouble taking credit for it. During this time I began to revisit the spiritual foundation that my mom and dad had given me as a kid.

There are no accidents in life. Shortly after being on "The Hour of Power," I got a call from Larry Hughes, president of William Morrow—the company that had published *The One Minute Manager*—asking if I would consider writing a book with Norman Vincent Peale. I said, "Is he still alive?" Larry said, "Not only is he alive, but he's fabulous." My parents had gone to Norman Vincent Peale's church before I was born, and Bob Schuller had modeled his church after Dr. Peale's *power of positive thinking* philosophy. In fact, Norman and his wife, Ruth, served on the board of the Crystal Cathedral for many years. Working with Norman Vincent Peale on *The Power of Ethical Management* and getting to spend time with Bob Schuller gave me a powerful one–two punch for looking at my relationship to the Lord.

Part of my recommitment to spiritual renewal involved taking our family to the Christmas pageant at the Crystal Cathedral. What an incredible spectacular it was, with live camels, donkeys, and flying angels! But the most moving part of the entire celebration was at the end, when the lights dimmed down and an incredible voice read "One Solitary Life." The story hit me like a ton of bricks, because it put in perspective that all this pushing in life for wealth, recognition, power, and status—all the things that people identify with success—doesn't really mean anything. What really matters is what you do for other people. You finally become an adult when you learn that life is about what you give rather than what you get.

In 1993 our good friends Pete and Donna Whiskerman sent "One Solitary Life" as part of their Christmas greeting. Although I'd heard it a number of times, the powerful impact of reading the words motivated me to put the story in my daily journal and read it every day. That's how important "One Solitary Life" became to me.

I often wondered who wrote "One Solitary Life" and if anybody had done anything with it in published form. We did a little digging and found that the essay was written by Dr. James Allan Francis as part of his 1926 book, *The Real Jesus*. About two years ago I had a wonderful visit with Mac Anderson, the founder of Successories, and we brainstormed about bringing "One Solitary Life" alive for everyone. Mac immediately went to work coordinating the design of this wonderful book.

Read "One Solitary Life" and put your life in perspective. You can make a difference, and it doesn't depend on how much money you make, how much you are recognized, or the power and status you receive. It's all about your relationship with the Lord and with those He puts in your life. May God bless your reading of this book.

KEN BLANCHARD

coauthor of *The One Minute Manager*®

and *The Servant Leader*

ONE SOLITARY LIFE

James Allan Francis

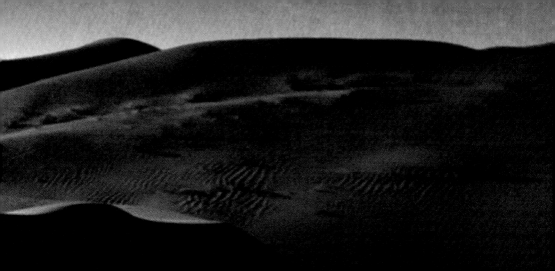

He was born in an obscure village
the child of a peasant woman.

He grew up in still another village

where He worked in a carpenter shop

until He was thirty, and then for three years

He was an itinerant preacher.

He never wrote a book.

He never held an office.

He never had a family.
He never owned a house.

He never went to college.

He never visited a big city.

He never traveled
two hundred miles
from the place
where He was born.

He did none of the things
one usually associates with greatness.

He had no credentials but Himself.

He was only thirty–three when
the tide of public opinion turned against Him.
His friends ran away.

He was turned over to His enemies
and went through the mockery of a trial.

He was nailed to a cross between two thieves

While He was dying
His executioners gambled for His clothing,
the only property He had on earth.

When He was dead
He was laid in a borrowed grave
through the pity of a friend.

Twenty centuries have come and gone,
and today Jesus is the central figure
of the human race,
the leader of mankind's progress.

All the armies that have ever marched

All the navies that have ever sailed

All the parliaments that have ever sat

All the kings that have ever reigned

                            put together

Have not affected the life
of mankind on this earth
as much as that
one solitary life.

Reflections

BY KEN BLANCHARD

I believe that Jesus was the greatest role model of all time. He was a master of the art of living. His One Solitary Life demonstrated that we don't need fame, money, and connections to live a life that really matters.

If we long to make a difference—and down deep, I think we all do—the example set by Jesus can guide our way.

BRINGING HEAVEN TO EARTH

"Let your light so shine before men,
that they see your good works,
and glorify your Father in heaven."

MATTHEW 5:16 NKJV

My good friend Bob Buford, founder of Leadership Network and author of *Halftime* and *Finishing Well*, says he believes all of us are going to face a "final exam" when we stand before God at the end of our lives. The two questions will be:

- What did you do about Jesus?
- What did you do with the resources you were given in life?

The first question is about faith and the second question is about works. Some people think that faith and works are in conflict. In some parts of the Bible it implies that faith is all that counts. In other parts, it says that faith without works is meaningless.

The well–known pastor Tony Evans from Dallas claims that faith and works are not really in conflict. He contends that faith gets you to heaven and it's your works that bring heaven down to earth. Jesus is concerned about both your faith and your works.

IT'S NOT ABOUT YOU

*"Come follow me," Jesus said,
"and I will make you fishers of men."*

MATTHEW 4:19 NIV

I ask people in my seminars whether they would like to make the world a better place for having lived here. Everybody raises their hands. Then I say to them, "What's your plan?" And everybody gets sheepish grins on their faces, because very few people have a plan.

And yet Jesus suggests a plan. The plan is to follow Him. The plan is to serve and help others. The plan is not about what you get in life; it's about what you give. It's about bringing heaven down to earth.

THE SECRET

※

The Jewish leaders saw that Peter and John
were not afraid to speak,
and they understood that these men
had no special training or education.
So they were amazed.
Then they realized that Peter and John had been with Jesus.

ACTS 4:13 NCV

Who could have foreseen that lowly fishermen of Galilee had the potential to become fearless apostles? Or that simple peasants could leave their nets behind to become founders of the church? Impossible . . . unthinkable . . . unless they came under the influence of that One Solitary Life. Even their enemies had to admit that the secret of these courageous, unschooled, ordinary men was that they "had been with Jesus." With His call to follow came His grace to enable them to make a difference in the world, and two thousand years later we still feel the impact of their lives. The same can be true of your life.

CHANGING YOUR FOCUS

"Whoever exalts himself will be humbled,
and he who humbles himself will be exalted."

MATTHEW 23:12 NKJV

Fred Smith, author of *You and Your Network*, says that people with humility don't deny their power; they just recognize that it passes through them, not from them.

For Jesus to work in your life so that you can make a difference, you have to be humble and realize from where your power comes. When you think life is all about you, your focus is on earthly success. You evaluate your life on how much money you have accumulated, the amount of recognition you have received, and the power and status you have earned. While there's nothing necessarily wrong with any of those things, a problem begins when you start to see yourself as those things. When that happens, your E.G.O. has taken over, and you've *Edged God Out.*

FROM SUCCESS
TO SIGNIFICANCE

"Life is not measured by how much one owns."
LUKE 12:15 NCV

Robert S. McGee, in his book *The Search for Significance*, says that if the devil has a formula for self-worth that he wants you to buy into, it would be: "Your self worth is equal to your performance plus the opinion of others."

If you are constantly looking to your performance or the opinions of others to make yourself feel good or worthwhile, you are constantly going to be chasing something you can never catch. Why? Because your performance will vary from day to day. That's a reality. And people are fickle. Their opinions will change.

What we have to do is change our focus from earthly success to spiritual significance and bask in the unconditional love of God.

GENEROSITY

"Give, and it will be given to you."

LUKE 6:38 NKJV

How can we attain spiritual significance? We can do it by *not* focusing on earthly successes such as wealth, recognition, power, and status. Instead, we should look at the opposite.

For example, rather than focus on the accumulation of wealth, we can focus on its opposite: *generosity*. And when we talk about generosity we're not only talking about giving treasure, but also giving our time, talent, and touch.

Charlie Tremendous Jones, author of *Life is Tremendous*, finds even the notion of giving to be ridiculous. "We should stomp out giving," he says, "Returning is the answer. After all, He owns it all—it's not really ours in the first place."

SERVICE

*"He who is greatest among you
shall be your servant."*

MATTHEW 23:11-12 NKJV

What's the opposite of recognition? It's *service*.

What Jesus wanted us to do was to serve. In His instructions to His first disciples on how they should behave when influencing others, Jesus sent a clear message to all those who would follow Him that leadership was to be first and foremost an act of service. No Plan B was implied or offered in His words. He placed no restrictions or limitations of time, place, or situation that would allow us to exempt ourselves from His command.

For the follower of Jesus, servant leadership isn't an option; it's a mandate. And that's the same for all aspects of our lives—we're here to serve, not to be served.

LOVE

❧

"'Love the Lord your God
with all your heart, all your soul,
and all your mind' . . .
Love your neighbor as you love yourself.'"
MATTHEW 22:36–40 NCV

What's the opposite of power and status? It's *loving relationships*.

This really hit me when I heard about the hundred-yard dash at the Special Olympics several years ago in Spokane, Washington. Nine contestants raced toward the finish line as fast as they could, given their physical disabilities. About a third of the way down the track, one of the boys fell and began to cry. While six of the other racers continued to push toward the finish line and possible victory, two of the youngsters stopped, turned around, headed back for their fallen competitor, and helped him up. The three boys held hands, walked down the track, and crossed the finish line together, well after the others had finished the race. The crowd rose and gave these youngsters a longer and louder ovation than the winner of the race.

Life is all about the choices we make as we interact with each other. Most of the youngsters chose to go for earthly success—victory in the race—while two tossed aside their own dreams in favor of compassion. The crowd responded with enthusiasm because we all yearn to live at a higher level, and these young people modeled what that means. They made a different choice.

Jesus wants us to make these kinds of choices. Life constantly presents us with opportunities to choose to love and serve one another. It's not about us. It's about reaching out and loving others.

YOU CAN MAKE A DIFFERENCE

*"Seek first the kingdom of God
and His righteousness,
and all these things shall be added to you."*

MATTHEW 6:33 NKJV

If you focus on earthly success, you'll never get to significance. But if you focus on spiritual significance, it's amazing how much true success can come your way. Mother Teresa could have cared less about money, recognition, power, and status, and yet those things and much more came to her and her ministry while she was focusing on significance.

Can One Solitary Life make a difference in your life? And through His energy, can you make a positive difference in the lives of others? You'd better believe it! But it will require a different focus. That means going beyond success to significance and ultimately, surrender. Go for it! And let Jesus make a difference through your life. God bless you.

One Solitary Life

JAMES A. FRANCIS

HE WAS BORN in an obscure village, the child of a peasant woman. He grew up in still another village, where He worked in a carpenter's shop until He was thirty. Then for three years He was an itinerant preacher. He never wrote a book, never held an office, never had a family or owned a house. He never went to college. He never visited a big city. He never traveled two hundred miles from the place where He was born. He did none of the things one usually associates with greatness. He had no credentials but Himself.

He was only thirty-three when the tide of public opinion turned against Him. His friends ran away. He was turned over to his enemies and went through the mockery of a trial. He was nailed to a cross between two thieves. While He was dying His executioners gambled for His clothing, the only property He had on earth. When He was dead He was laid in a borrowed grave through the pity of a friend.

Twenty centuries have come and gone, and today Jesus is the central figure of the human race and the leader of mankind's progress. All the armies that ever marched, all the navies that ever sailed, all the parliaments that ever sat, all the kings that ever reigned put together have not affected the life of mankind on this earth as much as that ONE SOLITARY LIFE.

Ken Blanchard is the chief spiritual officer of The Ken Blanchard Companies, a worldwide human resource development company. He is also cofounder of the Center for Faithwalk Leadership, a nonprofit ministry dedicated to inspiring and equipping people to Lead Like Jesus at work, home, and the community.

Few people have made a more positive and lasting impact on the day–to–day management of people and companies as Ken Blanchard. He is the author of several best–selling books, including the blockbuster international bestseller *The One Minute Manager*® and the giant business bestsellers *Raving Fans, Gung Ho!* and *Whale Done!* His coauthored books about Jesus as the ultimate leadership role model (*Leadership by the Book* and *The Servant Leader*) have ignited a Lead Like Jesus movement.

He and his wife, Margie, live in San Diego and work with their son Scott, daughter Debbie, and Debbie's husband, Humberto Medina.

For more information, please visit www.leadlikejesus.com or www.kenblanchard.com.

Mac Anderson is the founder of Successories®, Inc., the leader in designing and marketing products for motivation and recognition. Successories, however, is not the first success story for Mac Anderson. He was also the founder and CEO of McCord Travel, the largest travel company in the Midwest, and part owner/VP of sales and marketing for Orval Kent Food Company, the country's largest manufacturer of prepared salads. Mac's accomplishments in these three unrelated industries provide some insight into his passion and leadership skills.

Mac brings the same passion to his speaking and writing. He speaks to many corporate audiences on a variety of topics, including leadership, motivation, and team building.

He has written three books, *The Nature of Success, The Power of Attitude,* and *The Essence of Leadership,* and has coauthored *To a Child, Love is Spelled T-I-M-E* and *The Race.*

For more information, please visit www.simpletruths.com.

The Center for Faithwalk Leadership is a nonprofit ministry dedicated to inspiring and equipping people to Lead Like Jesus at work, home, and the community. The ministry offers seminars, learning materials, and simulcast Lead Like Jesus celebrations that are available through a satellite broadcasting system.

To learn more, visit www.leadlikejesus.com.

Or contact us at:
The Center for Faithwalk Leadership
1229 Augusta West Parkway
Augusta, GA 30909
800–383–6890
Fax: 760–489–1332

Simple Truths is a publishing company for gift books helping organizations to reinforce core values. The company also offers custom packaging and other personalization options for customer and employee gifts.

To learn more, visit www.simpletruths.com

Or contact us at:
Simple Truths
130 Washington Street
Dundee, Illinois 60118